Saving Frogs

Alan Lane
Virginia King

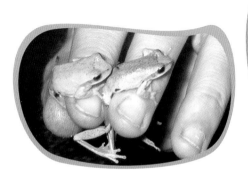

ETA
Cuisenaire

ETA Cuisenaire
800-445-5985 www.etacuisenaire.com

Saving Frogs

ISBN 978-0-7406-2774-3
ETA 303081

ETA/Cuisenaire • Vernon Hills, IL 60061-1862
800-445-5985 • www.etacuisenaire.com

Published by ETA/Cuisenaire® under license from Pearson Australia
(a division of Pearson Australia Pty Ltd)
All rights reserved.

Text © 2001 Alan Lane and Virginia King
Designer: Caroline Laird
Acknowledgments: Page 4, 10 (bottom right), 16, 17, Dr. Michael Mahony/
University of Newcastle; 28, Frank Filippi/copyright CSIRO; all other photos
including cover, Alan Lane and Virginia King.

Dr. Michael Mahony's work is supported by Earthwatch, an international
organization that supports many scientific research programs around the world.
The authors would like to thank Dr. Mahony and his team from the University of
Newcastle for their assistance in the creation of this book.

Printed in China (SWTC/08)

16 17 18 19   11 10 9 8

Contents

Saving Frogs

There used to be a lot of different kinds of frogs in the ponds and creeks around the world. People heard their croaking at night or when it rained. Then around 1980, people noticed that there weren't as many frogs as there used to be. Frogs seemed to be disappearing in many countries. Over the next ten years, many kinds of frogs became extinct and others became rare.

This Blue Mountains Tree Frog used to be very common. Now it is rare.

Scientists began to study the frogs to find out what the problem was. What could be killing the frogs? Where should the scientists start looking to find the answer? One team of scientists has been studying frogs for years. The leader of the team is Dr. Michael Mahony.

Dr. Mahony and his team are getting ready to study the frogs in some creeks. They are looking at a map of the area.

Steps for Saving Frogs

We are going on a field trip with Dr. Mahony and his team. We want to find out what is happening to the frogs in certain creeks. The creeks are in forests that are a long way from the city. The information that we collect about these frogs might help us figure out what is killing the frogs in many countries.

We keep studying the same creeks every year to see if the frogs are changing in any way. This information will tell us whether the number of frogs is getting larger or smaller, whether the frogs are breeding or not, and whether the frogs are healthy or sick.

Dr. Mahony and his team have been visiting the same creeks for several years so they can compare the information from year to year. There's a lot to find out and we're going to get wet!

Step 1

Prepare the Creek

We need to remember exactly where we find each frog. So, we measure the creek. We use markers to show different distances from the start. Then when we find a frog, we write down the number of the nearest marker. The markers also help us put the frog back exactly where we found it.

We measure the creek with a long tape measure.

We put markers on the trees to show the distance from the start. We work in the daytime, so we can see what we are doing.

step 2

Find the Frogs

Frogs hide in the daytime and come out at night to look for food and mates. In the area around the creek, each kind of frog chooses a different place to sit.

The Red-Eyed Green Tree Frog sits on a branch near the creek.

The Great Barred River Frog sits among the dead leaves near the water. Sometimes it is hard to see because its body has camouflage that matches the leaves.

The Dwarf Green Tree Frog calls for a mate while sitting on plants floating on the water.

The Whirring Tree Frog sits on reeds hanging over the water.

The Mountain Mist Frog makes a little burrow in the mud beside the water. (Read about how to find this frog on page 13.)

11

To find the frogs and study them, we go out in the dark with flashlights on our heads. Different frogs sit in different places. We have to use different ways to find them. Some of the frogs are very small, so we move carefully at all times.

If we move our flashlights slowly, we can find some frogs in the bushes and on the ground. We found this Eastern Pobblebonk Frog with a flashlight. Some frogs give away where they are because their eyes shine in the beam of light.

The frogs on the ground and in burrows can be hard to find because they are camouflaged or buried. To find these frogs, we try to make a sound like the frog! When the frog calls back, we move toward the sound. We keep calling and listening, moving closer and closer to the frog.

We are looking for a Mountain Mist Frog in its burrow by calling and listening. When we are sure where the frog is, we carefully remove the mud.

step 3

Look at the Frogs

When we catch each frog, we carefully put it in a bag.
We take it to Dr. Mahony and he looks at it closely.
Then we write down the answers to these questions.

What kind of frog is it?

We need to know how many kinds of frogs are in
this creek. Then we can check to see if the same
kinds of frogs are still in the creek each time we visit.
If one kind of frog starts to disappear, that is important
to know.

Whirring Tree Frogs

A Green Tree Frog

A Great Barred River Frog

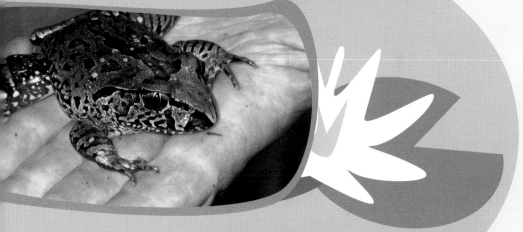

A Whistling Tree Frog

15

Is it male or female?

A group of frogs is healthy when there is a balance between males and females. If we find mostly males or mostly females, this may be a sign that something is wrong and that the frogs in the creek may be in danger.

Male frogs call to find mates. We found this male Bleating Tree Frog because it was calling.

Female frogs are much bigger than males. This female Bleating Tree Frog is looking plump because it is full of eggs.

Is it a young frog or an old frog?

In every creek, there should be frogs from each age group, from young to old. If we find that one age group is missing, this is a sign that something is wrong.

This "frogling" will soon lose its tail and become a young frog. A creek that is a healthy place for frogs has a lot of tadpoles and froglings.

Is the frog healthy or sick?

We look closely at each frog to see if it has an injury or any sign of disease. A frog may get bitten as it escapes from something that is trying to eat it. This is a normal danger in a frog's life. But sometimes a frog gets sick or dies for an unusual reason.

This Red-Backed Toadlet looks dead, but it's only pretending! When this frog thinks it is in danger, it plays dead by lying very still on its back. It shows its black and white belly.

We found some frogs with rashes on their skin. These frogs looked sick, and they died soon after.

If the team finds a dead frog, Dr. Mahony takes the body back to the laboratory to find out what killed it. Sick or dead frogs are hard to find, but they give us important clues about why some frogs are disappearing.

This Blue Mountains Tree Frog was dead. We found it near the creek. It had something wrong with its skin.

Step 4

Look at the Eggs and Tadpoles

We look for the eggs of all the different frogs we have found. Some frogs lay a lot of eggs and leave them to hatch. Other frogs lay a small number of eggs and guard them until they hatch.

We also catch tadpoles and count them. We compare the number of tadpoles this time with the number of tadpoles last time we came. This shows if there are any changes in the way the frogs are breeding in this creek.

Through the microscope, we can see if the eggs and tadpoles are growing normally.

We don't count all the tadpoles in the creek! We scoop a net through the water for 30 seconds and then lift it out. This is called sampling.

We count the tadpoles in the net. Then we put the tadpoles back in the water.

Step 5

Count and Measure the Frogs

We measure each frog to find out how long it is and weigh it to find out how heavy it is. Once we know its size, we can figure out its age. Each time we visit the creek, we compare the number of frogs and their ages. Then we can tell how long the frogs are living and if there are frogs of all ages in this creek.

Dr. Mahony measures each frog's body and head. Then he uses a scale to measure how heavy each frog is. The team writes down the information. Everyone gets to take a turn.

Record the Information

We write down all the information that we collect about the frogs and tadpoles.

Wolli Creek Thursday, April 21

Kind of Frog	Gender	Size of Frog			Place Found
		Weight (ounces)	Body Length (inches)	Head Width (inches)	(feet along creek)
Red-Eyed Green Tree Frog	Male	1.7	2.1	0.7	49
Great Barred River Frog	Male	2.3	3.1	1.3	236
Great Barred River Frog	Female	6.0	4.3	1.6	361

We compare this information with what we found on other visits to the creek. We look for any changes in the way the frogs are breeding, growing, and dying.

step 7
Put the Frogs Back

Frogs need to be where it's dark and wet. Also, they do not like being handled for too long. So as soon as we finish looking at a frog and measuring it, we put it back exactly where we found it.

The markers along the creek show us the exact place to put each frog back.

Study the Information

We compare the information we have collected with what we found on other visits to the creek. If we find changes in the numbers and kinds of frogs, we think about what could be causing the changes.

Dr. Mahony and his team spend time each day putting all the information together and thinking about what it means.

The information collected by Dr. Mahony and scientists in other countries shows that many kinds of frogs are healthy and happy. These frogs are not in danger. But the information also shows that some kinds of frogs are in danger of becoming extinct. Other frogs have already disappeared. Scientists want to find out what is killing these frogs and try saving them.

The Green and Golden Bell Frog is one kind of frog that is in danger. It has disappeared from most of the places where it used to live.

What Seems to Be Killing Some Frogs?

By studying frogs in many different countries, scientists like Dr. Mahony have learned that some frogs are dying from a fungus called the chytrid (say *KIT-rid*) fungus. Now scientists need to find out more about the chytrid fungus.

- Why is the chytrid fungus deadly to some frogs and not others?
- How can we protect frogs from the fungus?

Sometimes scientists found frogs that looked sick, like this one. Something was wrong with their skin, and they died. This frog has the chytrid fungus.

Taking Care of Frog Habitats

When people build houses, roads, and shopping malls, they fill in ponds, swamps, and creeks, and they cut down forests. Every time a frog habitat is destroyed, the number of frogs gets smaller. Soon there are not enough frogs left to breed and survive. The loss of habitat is another way that the animals become extinct.

Do you have a frog habitat near where you live? How could you help protect it?

You can help to save frogs, too.

- Keep garden fertilizers and poisons away from creeks and ponds.
- Find frog habitats and ask your town to look after them.
- Find out how to build a frog-friendly pond where you live.
- Listen to frogs and watch them, but do not catch them.

This small swamp is near houses and factories. The town put posts around it to show people that it is a frog habitat.